Martin Sherman

BENT

AMBER LANE PRESS

All rights whatsoever in this play are strictly
reserved and application for performance, etc.,
should be made before rehearsal to:
Margaret Ramsay Ltd.,
14A Goodwin's Court,
St Martin's Lane,
London WC2N 4LL.

No performance may be given unless a licence
has been obtained.

In the American territory please apply to:
Charles Hunt,
Fifi Oscard Associates,
19 West 44th Street,
New York, N.Y. 10036,
U.S.A.

First published in 1979, reprinted 1983, 1987
Amber Lane Press Ltd
Cheorl House
Church Street
Charlbury, Oxford OX7 3PR

Printed in Great Britain by
Bocardo Press Ltd, Didcot, Oxon.

Bent was first given a staged reading at the 1978 Eugene O'Neill playwrights' conference in Connecticut.

It received its world premiere at the Royal Court Theatre, London, on 3 May, 1979, with Ian McKellen as Max and Tom Bell as Horst.

On 4 July, 1979 it transferred to the Criterion Theatre, London. It was directed by Robert Chetwyn and designed by Alan Tagg, with the following cast:

MAX	Ian McKellen
HORST	Tom Bell
RUDY	Jeff Rawle
WOLF	Terence Suffolk
FREDDIE	Richard Gale
GRETA	Ken Shorter
VICTOR	Roger Dean
CORPORAL	
LIEUTENANT	Haydn Wood
GUARD ON TRAIN	
2ND LIEUTENANT	Jeremy Arnold
KAPO	
CAPTAIN	Peter Cellier
OFFICER	John Francis

Characters in order of appearance

MAX
RUDY
WOLF
LIEUTENANT
2ND LIEUTENANT
GRETA
VICTOR
FREDDIE
HORST
GUARD ON TRAIN
OFFICER
KAPO
CORPORAL
CAPTAIN

ACT ONE

SCENE ONE

The living room of an apartment. It is small and sparsely furnished. There is a table with plants on it. A door on the left leads to the outside hall. Nearby is an exit to the kitchen. On the right is an exit to the bedroom and nearby one to the bathroom.

MAX *enters, wearing a bathrobe. He is thirty-four. He is very hung over. He stares into space.*

MAX: Oh God!

[*He goes into the bathroom. Pause.*]

[*off*] Oh God!

[*He returns to the living room and sits down.* RUDY *enters, wearing a bathrobe. He is thirty and wears glasses. He carries a cup.*]

RUDY: Here.

[*He hands* MAX *the cup.* MAX *stares and doesn't take it.*]

Here. Coffee!

[MAX *takes the cup.*]

MAX: Thanks.

[*They kiss.* MAX *sips the coffee.*]

RUDY: It's late. It's almost three. We really slept. I missed class. I hate to dance when I miss class. Bad for the muscles. And there's no place to warm up at the club. I hate that night-club anyhow. The floor's no good. It's cement. You shouldn't dance on cement. It ruins my ankle. They've covered it with wood. Last night, before the show, I pounded on the wood — really hard — and I could hear the cement. I'm going to complain. I really am.

[*He goes into the kitchen.* MAX *sits in silence and stares.*]

MAX: Oh God.

[RUDY *returns from the kitchen with a jug of water and waters the plants.*]

RUDY: The plants are dying. The light's bad in this flat. I wish we had a decent place. I wish one of your deals would come through again. Oh, listen to me, wanting a bigger place. Rosen's gonna be knocking on our door any minute now, you know that, wanting his rent. We're three weeks overdue. He always comes on a Sunday. Slimy Jew, that's what he is, only cares about money — just what everyone always says about them. What's three weeks? He can wait. Well, at least I got the new job. I'll get paid on Thursday. If Greta keeps the club open. Business stinks. Well, I suppose it means I can't complain about the cement. The thing is, I don't want to dance with a bad ankle. More coffee?

[MAX *shakes his head 'yes'.* RUDY *goes into the kitchen.* MAX *stares into space. He puts his hand on his head and takes a deep breath, then closes his eyes.*]

MAX: One. Two. Three. Four. Five. [*He opens his eyes and takes another deep breath.*] Six. Seven. Eight. Nine. Ten.

[RUDY *returns from the kitchen and hands* MAX *another cup of coffee.* RUDY *resumes watering the plants.* MAX *watches him for a moment.*]

OK. Tell me.

RUDY: What?

MAX: You know.

RUDY: No.

MAX: Come on.

RUDY: I *don't* know. Listen, do you think I should ask Lena for the rent? She's such a good person. No feeling for music, though, which is daft, she's got such a good line. Perfect legs. Teddy wants to do a

dance for her in total silence. You think that's a
good idea? There's no place to do it, though.
There's no work. Lena lost that touring job. So she
must be broke. So she can't lend us the money. Want
some food?

MAX: Just tell me.

RUDY: What?

MAX: Must really be bad.

RUDY: What must?

MAX: That's why you won't tell me.

RUDY: Tell you what?

MAX: Don't play games.

RUDY: I'm not playing anything.

MAX: I'll hate myself, won't I? [*Silence.*] Won't I?

RUDY: I'll make something to eat.

MAX: Was I really rotten?

RUDY: Eggs.

MAX: I don't want eggs.

RUDY: Well, we're lucky to have them. I stole them from
the club. They don't need eggs. People go there to
drink. And see a terrific show — which is a bit sad
because the show's hopeless. You know, I'm so em-
barrassed, I have to think of other things while I'm
dancing. I have to think of grocery lists. And that's
cheating. If you're thinking of grocery lists, they
can tell out there that you're not thinking about
straw hats or water lilies — I mean, it really shows,
particularly when it's grocery lists. Your face looks
really depressed, when you can't afford groceries . . .

> [MAX *rises and puts his hand on* RUDY's
> *mouth.*]

MAX: Stop it.

> [RUDY *tries to speak.*]

Stop it!

> [*They struggle.* MAX *keeps his hand over*
> RUDY's *mouth.*]

I want to know what I did.

> [*He releases* RUDY. RUDY *smiles.*]

RUDY: I love you.
> [*He goes into the kitchen.*]

MAX: Rudy! Your plants. I'll pull the little buggers out unless you tell me.
> > [RUDY *comes back in.* MAX *stands over the plants.*]

RUDY: No you won't.

MAX: Like to bet? I did last month.

RUDY: You killed one. That was mean.

MAX: I'll do it again.

RUDY: Don't touch them. You have to be nice to plants. They can hear you and everything. [*to the plants*] He's sorry. He didn't mean it. He's just hung over.

MAX: What did I do?
> > [*Silence.*]

RUDY: Nothing much.

MAX: I can't remember a thing. And when I can't remember, it means . . .

RUDY: It doesn't mean anything. You drank a lot. That's all. The usual.

MAX: How'd I get this?
> > [*He pulls his robe off his shoulder and shows a mark on his skin.*]

RUDY: What's that?

MAX: Ouch! Don't touch it.

RUDY: I want to see it.

MAX: So *look*. You don't have to touch.

RUDY: What is it?

MAX: What does it look like? A big black and blue mark. There's another one here.
> > [*He shows a mark on his arm.*]

RUDY: Oh.

MAX: How did I get them?

RUDY: You fell.

MAX: How?

RUDY: Someone pushed you.

MAX: Who?

RUDY: Some bloke.

MAX: What bloke?

RUDY: Nicky's friend.

MAX: Who's Nicky?

RUDY: One of the waiters at the club.

MAX: Which one?

RUDY: The redhead.

MAX: I don't remember him.

RUDY: He's a little fat.

MAX: Why'd Nicky's friend push me?

RUDY: You asked Nicky to come home with us.

MAX: I did?

RUDY: Yes.

MAX: But he's *fat*.

RUDY: Only a little.

MAX: A threesome with a fat person?

RUDY: Not a threesome. A twelvesome. You asked *all* the waiters. All at the same time too. You were standing on a table, making a general offer.

MAX: Oh. Then what?

RUDY: Nicky's friend pushed you off the table.

MAX: And . . .

RUDY: You landed on the floor, on top of some boy in leather.

MAX: What was he doing on the floor?

RUDY: I don't know.

MAX: Was Greta mad?

RUDY: Greta wasn't *happy*. [*Pause.*] It was late. Almost everyone had gone. And you were very drunk. People like you drunk. [*Pause.*] I'll make some food.

MAX: I don't want food. Why didn't you stop me?

RUDY: How can I stop you?

MAX: Don't let me drink.

RUDY: Oh. Sure. When you're depressed?

MAX: Was I depressed?

RUDY: Of course.

MAX: I don't remember why.

RUDY: Then drinking worked, didn't it?

> [*He returns to the kitchen. A blond man* (WOLF) *enters, bleary-eyed, from the bedroom. He is in his early twenties. He is naked.*]

WOLF: Good morning.

> [*He stumbles into the bathroom.*]

MAX: Rudy!

RUDY: [*coming out of the kitchen*] What?

MAX: Who was that?

RUDY: Who was what?

MAX: That! That person!

RUDY: Oh. Yes. Blond?

MAX: Yes.

RUDY: And big?

MAX: Yes.

RUDY: That's the one you fell on.

MAX: The boy in leather?

RUDY: Yes. You brought him home.

> [*He goes into the kitchen.*]

MAX: Rudy! Your plants!

RUDY: [*returning from the kitchen*] You brought him home, that's all. He got you going. All that leather, all those chains. You called him your own little storm-trooper. You insulted all his friends. They left. I don't know why they didn't beat you up, but they didn't. They left. And you brought him home.

MAX: And we had a threesome?

RUDY: Maybe the two of you had a threesome. Max, there is no such thing. You pick boys up. You think you're doing it for me too. You're not. I don't like it. You and the other bloke always end up ignoring me anyhow. Besides, last night you and your own little storm-trooper began to get rough with each other, and I know pain is very chic just now, but I don't like it, 'cause pain hurts, so I went to sleep. [*He takes* MAX's *cup and pours the coffee onto the plants.*] Here Walter, have some coffee.

MAX: Walter?

RUDY: I'm naming the plants. They're my friends.

                    [*He goes into the kitchen.* WOLF *comes out
                    of the bathroom, wearing a towel. He grins
                    at* MAX.]

MAX: Rudy!

                    [RUDY *returns from the kitchen. He looks at*
                    WOLF.]

RUDY: Oh. There's a bathrobe in there — in the bedroom.

                    [WOLF *goes into the bedroom. Pause.*]

MAX: I'm sorry.

RUDY: It's OK.

MAX: I'm a rotten person. Why am I so rotten? Why do I
        do these things? He's gorgeous, though, isn't he? I
        don't remember anything. I don't remember what
        we did in bed. Why don't I ever remember?

RUDY: You were drunk. And high on coke.

MAX: That too?

RUDY: Yes.

MAX: Whose coke?

RUDY: Anna's.

MAX: I don't remember.

RUDY: You made arrangements to pick up a shipment to
        sell.

MAX: A *shipment*?

RUDY: Yes.

MAX: Christ! When?

RUDY: I don't know.

MAX: That can pay the rent for months.

RUDY: Anna will remember.

MAX: Right. Hey — rent. Maybe . . . do you think . . .?

RUDY: What?

MAX: We can ask him.

RUDY: Who?

MAX: Him!

RUDY: You must be joking.

MAX: Why?

RUDY: We don't know him.

MAX: I slept with him. I think. I wonder what it was like.

RUDY: You picked him up one night and you're going to
        ask him to lend you the rent?

MAX: Well, you know how I am.

RUDY: Yes.

MAX: I can talk people into things.

RUDY: Yes!

MAX: I can try.

RUDY: It won't work. He thinks you're rich.

MAX: Rich?

RUDY: You told him you were rich.

MAX: Wonderful.

RUDY: And Polish.

MAX: Polish!

RUDY: You had an accent.

> [RUDY *laughs and returns to the kitchen.* WOLF *walks out, in a short bathrobe. He stands and looks at* MAX. *There is an embarrassed silence.*]

MAX: Hello.

WOLF: Hello. The dressing gown is short. I look silly.

MAX: You look fine.

WOLF: Yes? You too.

> [*He goes to* MAX *and kisses him, then starts to pull* MAX's *robe off. He bites* MAX *on the chest.*]

> Ummm . . .

MAX: Hey. Not now.

WOLF: Later then.

MAX: Yes.

WOLF: In the country.

MAX: The country?

WOLF: Your voice is better.

MAX: Oh?

WOLF: You don't have an accent.

MAX: Only when I'm drunk.

WOLF: Oh.

MAX: Last night — was it good?

WOLF: What do you think?

MAX: I'm asking.

WOLF: Do you have to ask?

> [RUDY *comes in with a cup of coffee.*]

RUDY: Some coffee?

WOLF: Yes. Thank you.

> [RUDY *hands him the cup. Silence.*]

> This place . . .

MAX: Yes?

WOLF: It's really . . .

> [*He stops. Silence.*]

MAX: Small?

WOLF: Yes. Exactly.

MAX: I suppose it is.

WOLF: You people are strange, keeping places like this in town. I don't meet people like you too much. But you interest me, your kind.

MAX: Listen . . .

WOLF: Oh look, it doesn't matter, who you are, who I am. I'm on holiday. *That* matters. The country will be nice.

MAX: What's the country?

WOLF: The house. Your house. Your country house.

MAX: [*to* RUDY] My country house?

RUDY: Oh, that. I forgot to tell you about that. We're driving there this afternoon.

MAX: To our country house?

RUDY: *Your* country house.

MAX: How do we get there?

RUDY: Car.

MAX: Mine?

RUDY: Right.

MAX: Why don't we stay here?

WOLF: Don't make jokes. You promised me two days in the country.

MAX: Your name.

WOLF: Yes?

MAX: I forgot your name.

WOLF: Wolf.

MAX: Wolf?

WOLF: I didn't forget yours.

MAX: Look, Wolf, I don't have a car.

WOLF: Of course you do.

MAX: No.

WOLF: You showed me. In the street. Pointed it out.

MAX: Did I? It wasn't mine.

WOLF: Not yours?

MAX: No. I don't have a house in the country either.

WOLF: You do. You told me all about it.

MAX: I was joking.

WOLF: I don't like jokes. You don't want me with you, is
       that it? Maybe I'm not good enough for you. Not
       rich enough. My father made watches. That's not so
       wonderful. Is it, Baron?

                [*Pause.*]

MAX: Baron?

RUDY: Don't look at me. *That* one I didn't know about.

MAX: Baron.

                [*He begins to laugh. There is a loud knock
                at the front door.*]

RUDY: Rosen!

MAX: Shit.

WOLF: You like to laugh at me, Baron?

                [*The knocking continues.*]

MAX: Listen, Wolf, darling, you're really very sweet and
       very pretty and I like you a lot, but you see, I'm not
       very sweet, because I have a habit of getting drunk
       and stoned and grand and making things up.
       Believe me, I'm not a Baron. There is no country
       house. There is no money. I don't have *any* money.
       Sometimes I do. Sometimes I sell cocaine, some-
       times I find people to invest in business deals, some-
       times . . . well, I scrounge, see, and I'm good at it,
       and in a few weeks, I will have some money again.
       But right now, nothing. Rudy and I can't pay our
       rent. This rent. Right here. This bloody flat. That's
       all we have. And that man knocking at our door is
       our landlord. And he's going to throw us out.
       Because we can't pay our rent. Out into the streets,
       Wolf, the streets. Filled with filth, vermin. And lice.
       And . . . urine. Urine! Unless someone can help us
       out. Unless someone gives us a hand. *That's* the

truth. Look, you don't believe me, I'll show you.
Right out there we have, just like in the flicks, the
greedy landlord. [*He puts his hand on the door-
knob.*] Fanfare please.

> [RUDY *simulates a trumpet call.*]

Here he is, the one and only — Abraham Rosen!

> [MAX *swings the door open with a flourish.*
> *Two men are standing outside — Gestapo*
> *officers — in full Nazi uniform, both*
> *holding guns. The* LIEUTENANT *points to*
> WOLF.]

LIEUT: Him!

WOLF: No!

> [WOLF *throws the coffee cup at the* LIEU-
> TENANT *and runs into the bathroom. The*
> LIEUTENANT *and the* 2ND LIEUTENANT *run*
> *after him.* RUDY *starts towards the bath-*
> *room but* MAX *pulls him back.*]

MAX: Idiot! Run!

> [MAX *grabs* RUDY *and they run out of the*
> *front door.*]
>
> [*The lights black out on the left side of the*
> *stage. A shot rings out in the bathroom.*
> WOLF *screams.*]
>
> [*The lights rise on the left side of the stage*
> *as* GRETA *enters.* GRETA *is a man dressed as a*
> *woman. He wears a silver dress, high green*
> *leather boots, a top hat and carries a silver*
> *cane. He is both elegant and bizarre.*]
>
> [*The* LIEUTENANT *watches as the* 2ND LIEU-
> TENANT *drags* WOLF *out of the bathroom.*
> *He is bleeding but still alive. He looks up at*
> *the* LIEUTENANT *and crawls slowly towards*
> *him.*]

WOLF: Bastard!

LIEUT: Wolfgang Granz, we have an order for your arrest.
You resisted. Too bad.

> [*The* LIEUTENANT *grabs* WOLF *by the neck,*
> *takes out a knife, and slits his throat.*]

[GRETA *tugs at a rope above him and pulls
down a trapeze. He thrusts himself up onto
the trapeze bar and sits there.*]
[*A projection in the centre of the stage
reads:* BERLIN — 1934.]
[*Lights out on the apartment. Full spot-
light on* GRETA.]

SCENE TWO

GRETA *sits on the trapeze. He sings in a smoky,
seductive voice.*

GRETA: 'Streets of Berlin
           I must leave you soon
           Ah!
           Will you forget me?
           Was I ever really here?

           Find me a bar
           On the cobblestoned streets
           Where the boys are pretty.
           I cannot love
           For more than one day
           But one day is enough in this city.
           One day is enough in this city.

           Find me a boy
           With two ocean blue eyes
           And show him no pity.
           Take out his eyes
           He never need see
           How they eat you alive in this city.
           They eat you alive in this city.

           Streets of Berlin
           Will you miss me?
           Streets of Berlin
           Do you care?

Streets of Berlin
Will you cry out
If I vanish
Into thin air?'
[*Silence.*]
OK Victor, cut the spot.

> [*The spotlight dims. Lights rise on* GRETA's
> *Club. The stage is to the left.* GRETA's
> *dressing room is on the right. It has a chair
> facing a mirror, and a screen to change
> behind.*]

I want the song to be perfect tonight. Tomorrow, I
cut it.

> [VICTOR *comes out and helps* GRETA *off the
> trapeze.*]

Jesus Christ! Careful!

> [VICTOR *pulls the trapeze down.*]

Take some time off. We're opening late this
evening. [*Walking to the dressing room*] And
Victor! I don't want to be disturbed.

> [GRETA *enters the dressing room. The lights
> fade on the rest of the club.*]

My heroes! Where are you?

> [MAX *and* RUDY *come from behind the
> screen. They are dressed in trousers and
> shirts, pieces of nightclub costumes.* GRETA
> *looks at them.*]

> [MAX *sits on a stool, lost in thought.* GRETA
> *sits in the chair, adjusting his costume in
> the mirror.*]

I'm getting rid of all the rough songs. Who am I
kidding? I'm getting rid of the club. Well — maybe.
Maybe not. I'll turn it into something else. We'll
see.

RUDY: Is it safe?

GRETA: What?

RUDY: For us to go home?

GRETA: You fucking queers, don't you have any brains at
all? No, it's not safe.

RUDY: I want to go home.

GRETA: You can't. You can't go anywhere.

RUDY: I have to get my plants.

GRETA: Oh God! Forget your plants. You can't go home. You certainly can't stay here. And you can't contact friends, so don't try to see Lena, she's a nice girl, you'll get her into a lot of trouble. You understand? You have to leave Berlin.

RUDY: Why? I live here, I work here.

GRETA: No, you don't. You're sacked.

RUDY: I *don't* understand. What did we do? Why should we leave?

GRETA: Don't leave. Stay. Be *dead* queers. Who cares? I don't.

[MAX *looks up.*]

MAX: Who was he?

GRETA: Who was who?

MAX: The blond?

GRETA: Wolfgang Granz.

MAX: What's that mean?

GRETA: He was Karl Ernst's boyfriend.

MAX: Who's Karl Ernst?

GRETA: What kind of world do you live in? Aren't you boys ever curious about what's going on?

MAX: Greta, don't lecture. Who's Karl Ernst?

GRETA: Von Helldorf's deputy. You know Von Helldorf?

MAX: The head of the storm-troopers in Berlin.

GRETA: I don't believe it. You've actually *heard* of someone. Right. Second in command at the SA, immediately under Ernst Röhm.

RUDY: Oh. Ernst Röhm. I know him.

[MAX *and* GRETA *stare at him.*]

He's that fat queen, with those awful scars on his face, a real big shot, friend of Hitler's, runs around with a lot of beautiful boys. Goes to all the clubs. I sat at his table once. He's been *here* too, hasn't he?

MAX: Rudy, shut up.

RUDY: Why?

MAX: Just shut up. [*to* GRETA] So?

GRETA: So Hitler had Röhm arrested last night.

MAX: I don't believe it. He's Hitler's right-hand man.

GRETA: Was. He's dead. Just about anyone who's high up in the SA is dead. Your little scene on top of that table was *not* the big event of the evening. It was a bloody night. The city's in a panic. Didn't you see the soldiers on the streets — the SS? How'd you get here in your bathrobes? You're bloody lucky, that's all. The talk is that Röhm and his storm-troopers — Von Helldorf, Ernst, your blond friend — the lot — were planning a coup. I don't believe it. What the hell, let them kill each other, who cares? Except, it's the end of the club. As long as Röhm was around, a queer club was still OK. Anyhow, that's who you had — Wolfgang Granz. I hope he was a good fuck. He was a real dummy too, or didn't you notice? What's the difference? You picked up the wrong bloke, that's all.

RUDY: We can explain to somebody. It's not as if we knew him.

GRETA: Of course. Explain it all to the SS. You don't explain. Not any more. You know, you queers are not very popular anyhow. It was just Röhm keeping you all safe. Now you're like Jews. Unloved, darling, unloved.

RUDY: How about you?

GRETA: Me? Everyone knows I'm not queer. I've got a wife and kids. Of course that doesn't mean much these days, does it? But—I'm still not queer. As for this. [*He fingers his costume.*] I go where the money is.

MAX: [*getting up*] Money.

GRETA: Right.

MAX: Money. Ah! Greta!

GRETA: What?

MAX: How much?

GRETA: How much what?

MAX: How much did they give you?
                    [GRETA *laughs.*]

GRETA: Oh [*He takes out a roll of money.*] This much.

MAX: And you told them where Granz was?

GRETA: Told them darling! I showed them your building.

RUDY: Greta, you didn't.

GRETA: Why not? You don't play games with the SS. Anyway, it's just what he would do, your big shot here. He likes money too. He just isn't very good at it. I, on the other hand, have quite a knack. Here [*He holds out the money.*] Take it.

RUDY: No.

GRETA: It will help.

RUDY: We don't want it.

MAX: Shut up, Rudy.

RUDY: Stop telling me to . . .

MAX: Shut up! It's not enough.

GRETA: It's all they gave me.

MAX: We need more.

GRETA: So get more.

MAX: If they catch us, it won't help you.

GRETA: Oh ? A threat? [*Pause.*] I'll do you a favour. Take some more. [*He holds out some more money.*] Here. How's that? I've made a lot off your kind, so I'm giving a little back.

RUDY: Don't take it.

MAX: OK.

[*He takes the money.*]

GRETA: Now get out.

MAX: [*To* RUDY] Come on . . .

RUDY: Where? I'm not leaving Berlin.

MAX: We have to.

RUDY: We don't have to.

MAX: They're looking for us.

RUDY: But I live here.

MAX: Come on . . .

RUDY: I've paid up for dance class for the next two weeks. I can't leave. And my plants . . .

MAX: Jesus! Come on!

RUDY: If you hadn't been so drunk . . .

MAX: Don't.

RUDY: Why'd you have to take him home?

MAX: How do I know? I don't remember!

RUDY: You've ruined everything.

MAX: Right. I always do. So you go off on your own, OK? Go back to dance class. They can shoot you in the middle of an arabesque. Take half.
[*He holds out some money.*]

RUDY: I don't want it.

MAX: Then fuck it!
[*He starts to leave.*]

RUDY: Max!

GRETA: Max. He can't manage alone. Stick together.
[MAX *turns back.*]
Take his hand, darling.
[RUDY *takes* MAX's *hand.*]
That's right.

RUDY: Where are we going to go?

GRETA: Don't! Don't say anything in front of me. Get out.
[MAX *stares at* GRETA. *Then he tugs at* RUDY *and pulls him out of the room.* GRETA *removes his wig. He stares at his face in the mirror.*]

[*Blackout*]

SCENE THREE

Lights up on a park in Cologne.
*A middle-aged man (*FREDDIE*), well-dressed, sits on a bench. He is reading a newspaper.* MAX *enters. He sees the man and goes to the bench. The man looks up.*

FREDDIE: Sit down.
[MAX *sits.*]
Pretend we're strangers. Having a little conversation in the park. Perfectly normal. [*He folds the newspaper.*] Do something innocent. Feed the pigeons.

MAX: There aren't any pigeons.

FREDDIE: Here.

> [*He hands* MAX *an envelope.*]

MAX: You're looking well.

FREDDIE: You're looking older.

MAX: Everything in here?

FREDDIE: Your papers and a ticket to Amsterdam.

MAX: Just one?

FREDDIE: Yes.

MAX: Shit.

FREDDIE: Keep your voice down. Remember, we're strangers. Just a casual conversation. Perfectly normal.

MAX: One ticket. I told you on the phone . . .

FREDDIE: *One* ticket. That's all.

MAX: I can't take it. Damn. Here. [*He gives the envelope back.*] Thanks anyway.

> [*He gets up.*]

FREDDIE: Sit down. It wasn't easy getting new papers for you. If the family finds out . . .

> [MAX *sits.*]
>
> I have to be careful. They've passed a law you know. We're not allowed to be fluffs any more. We're not even allowed to kiss or embrace or fantasize. They can arrest you if you have fluff thoughts.
>
> [MAX *laughs.*]

MAX: Oh, Uncle Freddie.

FREDDIE: It's not funny.

MAX: It is.

FREDDIE: The family takes care of me. But you. Throwing it in everyone's face. No wonder they don't want anything to do with you. Why couldn't you have been quiet about it? Settled down, got married, paid for a few boys on the side. No one would have known. Ach! Take this.

MAX: I can't. Stop giving it to me.

> [*Silence.*]

FREDDIE: Look over there.

MAX: Where?

FREDDIE: Over there. See him?

MAX: Who?

FREDDIE: With the moustache.

MAX: Yes.

FREDDIE: Rather sweet.

MAX: Yes.

FREDDIE: Think he's a fluff?

MAX: I really don't know.

FREDDIE: You've been running for two years now. Haven't you? With that dancer. The family knows all about it. You can't live like that. Take this ticket.

MAX: I need two.

FREDDIE: I can't get two.

MAX: Of course you can.

FREDDIE: Yes. I think he is a fluff. You have to be so careful now. What is it? Do you love him?

MAX: What?

FREDDIE: The dancer.

MAX: Christ!

FREDDIE: Do you?

MAX: Don't be stupid. What's love? Love! I'm a grown-up now. I just feel responsible.

FREDDIE: Fluffs can't afford that kind of responsibility. Why are you laughing?

MAX: That word. Fluffs. Look, do you think it's been a holiday? We've tramped right across this country. We settle in somewhere, and then suddenly they're checking papers, and we have to leave — rather quickly. Now we're living outside Cologne, in the goddamn forest! In a colony of *tents* — can you believe that? *Me* in a tent! With hundreds of very boring unemployed people. Except most of them are just unemployed; they're not running from the Gestapo. I'm not cut out for this, Uncle Freddie. I was brought up to be comfortable. Like you. OK. I've been playing around for too long. You're right. The family and I should make up. So. How about a deal? *Two* tickets to Amsterdam. And two new sets

of identity papers. Once we get to Amsterdam, I'll
ditch him. And they can have me back.

FREDDIE: Maybe they don't want you back. It's been ten years.

MAX: They want me. It's good business. I'm an only son.
[*Pause.*] Remember that marriage father wanted to
arrange? Her father had button factories too, I just
read about her in the paper; she's an eligible
widow, living in Brussels. Make the arrangements
again. I'll marry her. Our button factories can sleep
with her button factories. It's a good deal. You
know it. And eventually, when all this blows over,
you can get me back to Germany. If I want a boy, I'll
rent him, like you. I'll be a discreet, quiet . . . fluff.
Fair enough? It's what father always wanted. Just
get us *both* out alive.

FREDDIE: I'll have to ask your father.

MAX: Do it. Then ask him.

FREDDIE: I can't do things on my own. Not now. [*He holds
out the envelope.*] Just this.

MAX: I can't take it.

FREDDIE: He's looking this way. He might be the police. No.
He's a fluff. He has fluff eyes. Still. You can't tell.
You'd better leave. Just be casual. Perfectly normal.
I'll ask your father.

MAX: Soon?

FREDDIE: Yes. Can I telephone you?

MAX: In the *forest?*

FREDDIE: Telephone me. On Friday.

> [FREDDIE *puts the envelope away.* MAX *gets
> up.*]

MAX: You're looking well, Uncle Freddie.

> [MAX *leaves.* FREDDIE *picks up his news-
> paper, glances at it, puts it down, and turns
> to look again at the man with the
> moustache.*]

[*Blackout*]

SCENE FOUR

The forest. In front of a tent. RUDY *sits in front of a fire. He has some apples, cheese and a knife. He calls back to the tent.*

RUDY: Cheese! Max!

> [MAX *comes out of the tent and sits down.*]

Here. Eat.

MAX: No.

RUDY: It's good.

MAX: I want some wine.

RUDY: There is no wine.

MAX: Where d'you get the cheese? Steal it?

RUDY: I don't steal. I dug a ditch.

MAX: You *what?*

RUDY: Dug a ditch. Right outside of Cologne. They're building a road. You can sign on each morning if you get there in time. They don't check your papers. It's good exercise too, for your shoulders. I'm getting nice shoulders. But my feet ... no more dancing feet. Oh God. Here. Have some.

MAX: I don't want to eat. You shouldn't have to dig ditches. I want some real food, for Christ's sake. I want some wine. [*He takes the cheese.*] Look at this cheese. It's awful. You don't know anything about cheese. Look at all these tents. There's no one to talk to in any of them. [*He eats a piece of cheese.*] It has no flavour.

RUDY: Then don't eat it. I'll eat it. I have apples too.

MAX: I hate apples.

RUDY: Then starve. What did you do today, while I was ditch digging?

MAX: Nothing.

RUDY: You had to do something.

MAX: Nothing.

RUDY: You weren't here when I got back.

MAX: Went to town.

RUDY: Have fun?

MAX: I'm working on something.
RUDY: Really?
MAX: Yes, a deal.
                    [*He takes an apple.*]
RUDY: Oh. A deal. Wonderful.
MAX: I might get us new papers and tickets to
       Amsterdam.
RUDY: You said that in Hamburg.
MAX: It didn't work out in Hamburg.
RUDY: You said that in Stuttgart.
MAX: Are you going to recite the list?
RUDY: Why not? I'm tired of your deals. You're right. This
       cheese is awful. I don't want to eat it.
                    [*He pushes the food aside.*]
MAX: You have to eat.
RUDY: Throw it out.
MAX: You'll be ill if you don't eat.
RUDY: So what?
MAX: All right. Be ill.
RUDY: No. I don't want to be ill. [*He eats a piece of cheese.*]
       If I'm ill, you'll leave me behind. You're just
       waiting for me to be ill.
MAX: Oh — here we go.
RUDY: You'd love it if I died.
MAX: Rudy!
RUDY: I know you would. Cheese makes me thirsty. Why
       didn't *you* buy wine?
MAX: I don't have any money. *You* dug the ditch.
RUDY: Of course. I dug the ditch. *I* make the money. If you
       call it money. You know how much they paid me?
       Enough for cheese and apples. You know what I
       keep asking myself?
MAX: What?
RUDY: If we had just talked to the SS that day and
       explained everything — could it have been worse
       than this?
MAX: Maybe not.
RUDY: Maybe not? You're supposed to say yes, *much*

worse. Don't tell me maybe not. I'll kill myself if I believe maybe not. That's what you want. You want me to kill myself.

MAX: I just want to get us out of here. These awful tents. There's no air. We're *in* the air, but there's still no air. I can't breathe. I've got to get us across the border.

RUDY: Why don't we just cross it?

MAX: What do you mean?

RUDY: This bloke, on the job today, was telling me it's easy to cross the border.

MAX: Oh, yes, it's simple. You just walk across. Of course, they shoot you.

RUDY: He said he knew spots.

MAX: Spots.

RUDY: Spots to get through. I told him to come talk to you.

MAX: Here?

RUDY: Yes.

MAX: I told you we don't want anyone to know we're here, or that we're trying to cross the border. How can you be so thick?

RUDY: I'm not thick.

MAX: He could tell the police.

RUDY: OK. So I *am* thick. Why don't we try it anyway?

MAX: Because . . .

RUDY: Why?

MAX: I'm working on something.

RUDY: Who with?

MAX: I can't tell you.

RUDY: Why not?

MAX: It spoils it. I can't talk about it before it happens. Then it won't happen. I'm superstitious.

RUDY: Then why'd you bring it up?

MAX: So you'd know that . . .

RUDY: What?

MAX: That I'm trying.

RUDY: This is madness. We're in the middle of the jungle . . .

MAX: Forest.

RUDY: Jungle. I'm a dancer, not Mowgli. I can't dance any
more. I've walked my feet away. But you don't
mind. You're working on something. You worked
on something in Berlin, you work on something in
the jungle.

MAX: Forest.

RUDY: Jungle. I want to get out of here. I could have. I met
a man in Frankfurt. You were in town 'working on
a deal'. He gave me a lift. He was an old man, rich
too. He was numb on his left side, he must have had
a stroke, he shouldn't have been driving. I could
have stayed with him. I could have got him to get
me out of the country. He really fancied me, I could
tell. But no, I had to think about you. It wasn't fair
to *you*. I'm thick, you're right. You would have
grabbed the chance. You're just hanging around,
waiting for me to die. I think you've poisoned the
cheese.

MAX: It's *your* cheese. Choke on it. Please, choke on it. I
can't tell you how much I want you to choke on it.
Christ! [*He picks up a knife and cuts the apple into
pieces.*] Listen . . . I think I *can* get us out of here.
Just hold on.

RUDY: What are you working on? Who with?

MAX: No.

RUDY: Come on.

MAX: No. Absolutely not! Trust me, just trust me.

RUDY: Why should I?
            [MAX *throws the knife down and gets up.*]
Where are you going?

MAX: I have to get out of here. I can't breathe. I'm going
for a walk.

RUDY: You can't. There's no place to walk. Just tents and
jungle.

MAX: I've got a temperature.

RUDY: What?

MAX: I've got a temperature! I'm burning.

RUDY: It's a trick.

> [*He gets up and goes to him. He tries to feel his forehead.* MAX *pulls away.*]

MAX: I know. I'm lying. Get away.

RUDY: Let me feel. [*He feels* MAX's *forehead.*] You have got a temperature.

MAX: It's the cheese. You poisoned *me*. What the hell. I'll die in the jungle.

> [*He sits down again.*]

RUDY: Forest.

> [*He sits down. Silence.*]

MAX: Well . . . what do we talk about now?

RUDY: I don't know.

> [*Silence.*]

MAX: Remember cocaine?

RUDY: Yes.

MAX: I'd like cocaine.

RUDY: Yes.

MAX: What would you like?

RUDY: New glasses.

MAX: What?

RUDY: My eyes have changed. I need a new prescription. I'd like new glasses.

MAX: In Amsterdam.

RUDY: Sure.

MAX: In *Amsterdam*. Cocaine and new glasses. Trust me. Plants. You'll have plants. Wonderful Dutch plants. And Dutch dance classes. Your feet will come back. And you won't dig ditches. You'll have to give up your new shoulders though. And you know what? We can buy a Dutch dog. Everyone should have a dog. I don't know why we didn't have a dog in Berlin. We'll have one in Amsterdam. [*Silence.*] Trust me.

> [RUDY *looks at* MAX *and smiles. Silence.*]
> Well? What do we talk about now?

RUDY: Let's sing.

MAX: Sing?

RUDY: Well, we're sitting around a campfire; that's when people sing.

MAX: You think they sing in The Hitler Youth?

RUDY: I don't know.

MAX: They always sit around campfires.

RUDY: I never joined. How're you feeling?

MAX: Burning.

> [RUDY *touches* MAX's *forehead. He keeps his hand there.*]

Don't.

RUDY: I'm sorry, Max.

> [*He strokes* MAX's *forehead.*]

MAX: Don't.

RUDY: I really love you.

MAX: Don't! [*He pulls* RUDY's *hand away.*] If they see us . . . from the other tents . . . they're always looking . . . they could throw us out . . . for touching . . . we have to be careful . . . we have to be very careful . . .

RUDY: OK.

> [*Pause. He starts to sing.*]

'Streets of Berlin
I must leave you soon
Ah!'

MAX: What are you doing?

RUDY: Singing. This must be the way The Hitler Youth does it. They sing old favourites. I'm sure they're not allowed to touch either.

MAX: Don't be so sure.

RUDY: Well, it's unfair if they could, and we can't.

> [*He starts to sing again.*]

'Streets of Berlin
I must leave you soon
Ah!'

> [MAX *takes* RUDY's *hand, holds it on the ground where it can't be seen, and smiles.*]

MAX: Shh!

> [*They laugh. They both sing.*]

RUDY: } 'Find me a bar
MAX: } On the cobblestoned streets.

Where the boys are pretty.

> I cannot love
> For more than one day
> But one day is enough in this city.
> One day is enough in this city.'

1ST VOICE: [*from the darkness*] There! That's them!

> [*A bright light shines on* MAX *and* RUDY.]

2ND VOICE: [*from the darkness*] Maximilian Berber. Rudolph
Hennings. Hands high in the air. You are under
arrest.

[*Blackout*]

SCENE FIVE

*A train whistle is heard. Sound of a train running
through the night. A train whistle again.*
*A circle of light comes up. It is a prisoner transport
train. We see one small corner. Five prisoners are in
the light — two men in civilian dress, then* RUDY
and MAX, *then a man wearing a striped uniform
with a pink triangle sewn onto it.*
A GUARD *walks through the circle of light. He
carries a rifle. Silence.*

RUDY: Where do you think they're taking us?

> [*Silence. The other prisoners look away.
> The* GUARD *walks through the circle of
> light. Silence.*]

> [*to the prisoner next to him*] Did you have a trial?

> [*The prisoner doesn't answer.*]

MAX: Rudy!

> [*Silence.* RUDY *and* MAX *look at each other.
> They are both terrified.* RUDY *starts to ex-
> tend his hand, then withdraws it. A scream
> is heard — off, beyond the circle.* RUDY *and*
> MAX *look at each other, then turn away.
> Silence.*]

> [*The* GUARD *walks through the circle of
> light. Silence. Another scream. Silence.*]

[*The* GUARD *walks through the circle of light.*]

[*An* SS OFFICER *enters. The circle slightly expands. The* OFFICER *looks at the prisoners one by one. He stops at* RUDY.]

OFFICER: Glasses. [*Silence.*] Give me your glasses.

[RUDY *hands the* OFFICER *his glasses. The* OFFICER *examines them.*]

Horn-rimmed. Intelligentsia.

RUDY: What?

[*The* OFFICER *smiles.*]

OFFICER: Stand up.

[*The* GUARD *pulls* RUDY *up.*]

Step on your glasses.

[RUDY *stands — petrified.*]

Step on them.

[RUDY *steps on the glasses.*]

Take him.

RUDY: Max!

[RUDY *looks at* MAX. *The* GUARD *pulls* RUDY *off — out of the circle. The* OFFICER *smiles.*]

OFFICER: Glasses.

[*He kicks the glasses away.*]

[*The* OFFICER *leaves the circle of light. The light narrows.* MAX *stares ahead.*]

[*The* GUARD *walks through the circle of light. Silence. A scream is heard — off, beyond the circle.* RUDY'S *scream.* MAX *stiffens. Silence.* RUDY *screams again.* MAX *moves, as to get up. The man wearing the pink triangle* (HORST) *moves towards* MAX. *He touches him.*]

HORST: Don't.

[*He removes his hand from* MAX *and looks straight ahead.*]

The GUARD *walks through the circle of light.*]

Don't move. You can't help him.

[RUDY *screams. Silence.*]
[*The* GUARD *walks through the circle of light.*]

MAX: This isn't happening.

HORST: It's happening.

MAX: Where are they taking us?

HORST: Dachau.

MAX: How do you know?

HORST: I've been through transport before. They took me to Cologne for a propaganda film. Pink triangle in good health. Now it's back to Dachau.

MAX: Pink triangle? What's that for?

HORST: Queer. If you're queer, that's what you wear. If you're a Jew, a yellow star. Political — a red triangle. Criminal — green. Pink's the lowest.
[*He looks straight ahead.*]
[*The* GUARD *walks through the circle of light.* RUDY *screams.* MAX *starts.*]

MAX: This isn't happening.
[*Silence.*]
This can't be happening.
[*Silence.*]

HORST: Listen to me. If you survive the train, you stand a chance. Here's where they break you. You can do nothing for your friend. Nothing. If you try to help him, they will kill you. If you try to care for his wounds, they will kill you. If you even *see* — see what they do to him, *hear* — hear what they do to him — they will kill you. If you want to stay alive, he cannot exist.
[RUDY *screams.*]

MAX: It isn't happening.
[RUDY *screams.*]

HORST: He hasn't a chance. He wore glasses.
[RUDY *screams.*]
If you want to stay alive, he cannot exist.
[RUDY *screams.*]
It *is* happening.
[HORST *moves away. The light focuses in*

> on MAX's face. RUDY *screams.* MAX *stares
> ahead, mumbling to himself.*]

MAX: It isn't happening ... it isn't happening ...

> [*The* GUARD *drags* RUDY *in.* RUDY *is semi-
> conscious. His body is bloody and
> mutilated. The* GUARD *holds him up. The*
> OFFICER *enters the circle.* MAX *looks away.
> The* OFFICER *looks at* MAX. MAX *is still
> mumbling to himself.*]

OFFICER: [*to* MAX] Who is this man?

MAX: I don't know.

> [MAX *stops mumbling. He looks straight
> ahead.*]

OFFICER: Your friend?

> [*Silence.*]

MAX: No.

> [RUDY *moans.*]

OFFICER: Look at him.

> [MAX *stares straight ahead.*]

Look!

> [MAX *looks at* RUDY. *The* OFFICER *hits*
> RUDY *on the chest.* RUDY *screams.*]

Your friend?

MAX: No.

> [*The* OFFICER *hits* RUDY *on the chest.* RUDY
> *screams.*]

OFFICER: Your friend?

MAX: No.

> [*Silence.*]

OFFICER: Hit him.

> [MAX *stares at the* OFFICER.]

Like this.

> [*The* OFFICER *hits* RUDY *on the chest.* RUDY
> *screams.*]

Hit him.

> [MAX *doesn't move.*]

Your friend?

> [MAX *doesn't move.*]

Your friend?

MAX: No.

>[MAX *closes his eyes. He hits* RUDY *on the chest.* RUDY *screams.*]

OFFICER: Open your eyes.

>[MAX *opens his eyes.*]

Again.

>[MAX *hits* RUDY *in the chest.*]

Again!

>[MAX *hits* RUDY *again and again and again . . .*]

Enough.

>[*The* OFFICER *pushes* RUDY *down to the ground, at* MAX's *feet.*]

Your friend?

MAX: No.

>[*The* OFFICER *smiles.*]

OFFICER: No.

>[*The* OFFICER *leaves the circle of light. The* GUARD *follows him.*]
>
>[*The light focuses in — on* MAX's *face. The train is heard running through the night. The train whistles.* RUDY *is heard — moaning — and calling* MAX's *name.* MAX *stares ahead.* RUDY *calls* MAX's *name. The name merges with the whistle.* MAX *takes a deep breath.* RUDY *calls* MAX's *name.*]

MAX: One. Two. Three. Four. Five. [*He takes another deep breath.*] Six. Seven. Eight. Nine. Ten.

>[RUDY *is silent.* MAX *stares ahead.*]

[*Blackout*]

SCENE SIX
Lights up, on one side of the stage. A large barrel is on the ground. A prisoner-foreman (KAPO) stands behind the barrel, with a huge ladle. He stirs it. The KAPO wears a green triangle on his prison uniform. Prisoners come up, one by one, with bowls in their hand, to be fed. They all wear prison uniforms.

KAPO: It's soup tonight.
> [*A prisoner with a yellow star enters. The* KAPO *stirs the soup.*]

Here. Let me stir it. Get the meat. There.
> [*He fills the prisoner's bowl. The prisoner leaves. A prisoner with a red triangle enters. The* KAPO *stirs the soup.*]

Here. Lots of vegetables.
> [*He fills the prisoner's bowl. The prisoner leaves.* HORST *enters. The* KAPO *does not stir the soup.*]

Here.
> [*He fills* HORST's *bowl.*]

HORST: Soup.

KAPO: What?

HORST: Only soup. You skimmed it from the top. There's nothing in it but water. No meat, no vegetables. Nothing.

KAPO: Take what you get.
> [HORST *reaches for the ladle.*]

HORST: Give me some meat.
> [*The* KAPO *pushes him back.*]

KAPO: Fucking queer! Take what you get!

[*Blackout*]

[*Lights rise on other side of the stage. A tight little corner at the end of the barracks.* HORST *crawls in and sits huddled with his bowl. He drinks the soup.* MAX *enters, crawling in next to* HORST. *He carries a bowl. He wears the prison uniform. On it is a yellow star.*]

MAX: Hello.
> [HORST *looks at him but says nothing.* MAX *holds up his bowl.*]

Here.

HORST: Leave me alone.

MAX: I got extra. Some vegetables. Here.

[*He drops some vegetables from his bowl into* HORST's *bowl.*]

HORST: Thanks.

[*They eat in silence.* HORST *looks up. He stares at* MAX's *uniform.*]

Yellow star?

MAX: What?

HORST: Jew?

MAX: Oh. Yes.

HORST: I wouldn't have thought it.

[*Silence.*]

I'm sorry about your friend.

MAX: Who?

HORST: Your friend.

MAX: Oh.

[*Silence.*]

HORST: It's not very sociable in these barracks. [*He laughs.*] Is it?

MAX: It's all right.

HORST: Right. You got a yellow star.

MAX: [*pointing to* HORST's *pink triangle*] How'd you get that?

HORST: I signed a petition.

MAX: And?

HORST: That was it.

MAX: What kind of petition?

HORST: For Magnus Hirschfield.

MAX: Oh yes. I remember him. Berlin.

HORST: Berlin.

MAX: He wanted to . . .

HORST: Make queers legal.

MAX: Right. I remember.

HORST: Looked like he would too, for a while. It was quite a movement. Then the Nazis came in. Well. I was a nurse. They said a queer couldn't be a nurse. Suppose I had to touch a patient's penis! God forbid. They said rather than be a nurse, I should be a prisoner. A more suitable occupation. So. That's

how I got my pink triangle. How'd you get the
yellow star?

MAX: I'm Jewish.

HORST: You're not Jewish, you're a queer.

[*Silence.*]

MAX: I didn't want one.

HORST: Didn't want what?

MAX: A pink triangle.

HORST: Didn't *want* one?

MAX: You told me it was the lowest.

HORST: In here, it is.

MAX: So I didn't want one.

HORST: So?

MAX: So I worked a deal.

HORST: A deal?

MAX: Yes. I'm good at that.

HORST: With the Gestapo?

MAX: Yes.

HORST: You're full of shit.

[*Silence.*]

MAX: I'm going to work a lot of deals. They can't keep us
here forever. Sooner or later they'll release us. I'm
only under protective custody, that's what they told
me. I'm going to stay alive.

HORST: I don't doubt it.

MAX: Sure. I'm good at that.

HORST: Thanks for the vegetables.

[*He starts to crawl away.*]

MAX: Where you going?

HORST: To sleep. We get up at four in the morning. I'm on
stone detail. I chop stones up. It's fun. Excuse me
. . .

MAX: Don't go.

HORST: I'm tired.

MAX: I don't have anyone to talk to.

HORST: Talk to your rabbi.

MAX: I'm not Jewish.

HORST: Then why are you wearing that?

MAX: It's better to be a Jew than a queer. In this place.

HORST: I think it's relative.

MAX: You told me pink was the lowest.

HORST: It is, but only because the *other* prisoners hate us so
         much. Except for a queer, no-one is treated worse
         than a Jew.

MAX: I got meat in my soup.

HORST: Good for you.

MAX: I'm going to stay alive.

HORST: Good. You do that.

MAX: Don't go.

HORST: Look, friendships last about twelve hours in this
         place. We had ours on the train. Why don't you go
         and bother someone else.

MAX: You didn't think I'd make it, did you? Off the train.

HORST: I wasn't sure.

MAX: I'm going to stay alive.

HORST: Yes.

MAX: Because of you. You told me how.

HORST: Yes. [*Pause.*] I did. [*Pause.*] I'm sorry.

MAX: About what?

HORST: I don't know. Your friend.

MAX: Oh. [*Silence.*] He wasn't my friend.
                      [*Silence.*]

HORST: You should be wearing a pink triangle.

MAX: I made a deal.

HORST: You don't make deals here.

MAX: I did. I made a deal.

HORST: Yes.
                      [*He starts to leave again.*]

MAX: They said if I . . . I could . . . they said . . .

HORST: What?

MAX: Nothing.
                      [HORST *crawls past* MAX.]
         I could prove . . . I don't know how . . .

HORST: What?
                      [*He stops and sits next to* MAX.]

MAX: Nothing.

[*Silence.*]

HORST: Try. [*Silence.*] I think you'd better. [*Silence.*] Try to
tell me.

MAX: Nothing.

[*Silence.*]

HORST: OK.

[*He moves away.*]

MAX: I made ... they took me ... into that room ...

[HORST *stops.*]

HORST: Where?

MAX: Into that room.

HORST: On the train?

MAX: On the train. And they said ... prove that you're ...
and I did ...

HORST: Prove that you're what?

MAX: Not.

HORST: Not what?

MAX: Queer.

HORST: How?

MAX: Her.

HORST: Her?

MAX: They said, if you ... and I did ...

HORST: Did what?

MAX: Her. Made ...

HORST: Made what?

MAX: Love.

HORST: Who to?

MAX: Her.

HORST: Who was she?

MAX: Only ... maybe ... maybe only thirteen ... she was
maybe ... she was dead.

HORST: Oh.

MAX: Just. Just dead, minutes ... bullet ... in her ... they
said ... prove that you're ... and I did ... prove that
you're ... lots of them, watching ... drinking ...
"He's a bit bent," they said, "he can't ..." But I did
...

HORST: How?

MAX: I don't ... I don't ... know. I wanted ...

HORST: To stay alive.

  MAX: And there was something . . .

HORST: Something . . .

  MAX: Exciting . . .

HORST: Oh God.

  MAX: I hit him, you know. I kissed her. Dead lips. I killed him. Sweet lips. Angel.

HORST: God.

  MAX: She was . . . like an angel . . . to save my life . . . just beginning . . . her breasts . . . just beginning . . . they said he can't . . . he's a bit bent . . . but I did . . . and I proved . . . I proved that I wasn't . . . [*Silence.*] And they enjoyed it.

HORST: Yes.

  MAX: And I said, "I'm not queer." And they laughed. And I said, "Give me a yellow star." And they said, "Sure, make him a Jew. He's not queer." And they laughed. They were having fun. But . . . I . . . got . . . my . . . star . . .

HORST: [*gently*] Oh yes.

  MAX: I got my star.

HORST: Yes.

> [*He reaches out and touches* MAX's *face.*]

  MAX: Don't do that! [*He pulls away.*] You mustn't do that. For your own sake. You mustn't touch me. I'm a rotten person.

HORST: No.

> [*He touches* MAX *again.* MAX *hits him.*]

  MAX: Rotten.

> [HORST *stares at* MAX.]

HORST: No.

> [HORST *crawls away and leaves.* MAX *is alone. He takes a deep breath. He closes his eyes then takes another deep breath. He opens his eyes.*]

  MAX: One. Two. Three. Four. Five. [*He takes another deep breath.*] Six. Seven. Eight. Nine. Ten.

> [*Blackout*]

ACT TWO

SCENE ONE

One month later.

*A large fence extends across the stage. In front of the
fence, on one side, lies a pile of rocks. On the other
side — far over — a deep pit.*

*MAX is moving rocks. He carries one rock from the
pile to the other side, and starts a new pile. He
returns and takes another rock. The rocks are
carried one by one. He wears a prison hat. A*
CORPORAL *enters with* HORST. HORST *also wears a
prison hat. The* CORPORAL *is very officious.*

CORPORAL: Here. You will work here.

HORST: Yes sir.

CORPORAL: He'll explain.

HORST: Yes sir.

CORPORAL: I'm up there.

[*He points off and up.*]

HORST: Yes sir.

CORPORAL: I see everything.

HORST: Yes sir.

CORPORAL: No slacking.

HORST: No sir.

CORPORAL: I see everything.

HORST: Yes sir.

CORPORAL: [*to* MAX] You.

[MAX *puts down his rock.*]

MAX: Yes sir.

CORPORAL: Tell him what to do.

MAX: Yes sir.

CORPORAL: No slacking.

MAX: No sir.

CORPORAL: I see everything.

MAX: Yes sir.

CORPORAL: [*to* HORST] You.

HORST: Yes sir.

CORPORAL: Every two hours there is a rest period.

HORST: Yes sir.

CORPORAL: For three minutes.

HORST: Yes sir.

CORPORAL: Stand at attention.

HORST: Yes sir.

CORPORAL: Don't move.

HORST: No sir.

CORPORAL: Rest.

HORST: Yes sir.

CORPORAL: Three minutes.

HORST: Yes sir.

CORPORAL: A bell rings.

HORST: Yes sir.

CORPORAL: [*to* MAX] You.

MAX: Yes sir.

CORPORAL: Explain it to him.

MAX: Yes sir.

CORPORAL: No slacking.

MAX: No sir.

CORPORAL: [*to* HORST] You.

HORST: Yes sir.

CORPORAL: When the bell rings.

HORST: Yes sir.

CORPORAL: Don't move.

HORST: No sir.

CORPORAL: Three minutes.

HORST: Yes sir.

CORPORAL: He'll explain.

HORST: Yes sir.

CORPORAL: [*to* MAX] You.

MAX: Yes sir.

CORPORAL: You're responsible.

MAX: Yes sir.

CORPORAL: I'm up there.

MAX: Yes sir.

CORPORAL: [*to* HORST] You.

HORST: Yes sir.

CORPORAL: I see everything.

HORST: Yes sir.

> [*The* CORPORAL *leaves.* HORST *watches carefully until he has gone.*]
>
> We had a boy like that in school. Used to lead us in 'Simon Says'.

MAX: OK. I'll explain.

HORST: OK.

MAX: We have to move rocks.

HORST: Yes sir.

MAX: You see those . . .

HORST: Yes sir.

MAX: You take one rock at a time.

HORST: Yes sir.

MAX: And move it over there.

HORST: Yes sir.

MAX: And then when the entire pile is over there, you take one rock at a time, and move it back.

> [HORST *looks at* MAX. *Silence.*]

HORST: And move it back?

MAX: Yes.

HORST: We move the rocks from there to there, and then back from there to there?

MAX: Yes sir.

HORST: Why?

MAX: Start moving. He's watching.

> [MAX *continues to move rocks.* HORST *does the same. They do so in different rhythms, at times passing each other.*]

HORST: OK.

MAX: It's supposed to drive us mad.

HORST: These are heavy!

MAX: You get used to it.

HORST: What do you mean, drive us mad?

MAX: Just that. It makes no sense. It serves no purpose. I worked it out. They do it to drive us mad.

HORST: They probably know what they're doing.

MAX: No, they don't. I worked it out. It's the best job to
have. That's why I got you here.

HORST: What!

[*He puts down his rock.*]

MAX: Don't stop. Keep moving.

[HORST *picks up the rock and moves it.*]

A couple more things. That fence.

HORST: Yes.

MAX: It's electric. Don't touch it. You fry.

HORST: I won't touch it.

MAX: And over there — that pit.

HORST: Where?

MAX: There.

HORST: Oh yes. It smells awful.

MAX: Bodies.

HORST: In the pit?

MAX: Yes. Sometimes we have to throw them in.

HORST: Oh. Well, it will break the routine. What do you
mean you got me here?

MAX: Don't walk so fast.

HORST: Why?

MAX: You'll tire yourself. Pace it. Nice and slow.

HORST: OK. This better?

MAX: Yes. Sometimes they let us change the pattern.

HORST: That's kind of them. What do you mean you got me
here?

MAX: I worked a deal.

HORST: I don't want to hear.

[*Silence.*]

Yes, I do. What's going on? You *got* me here? What
right do you have . . .?

MAX: Careful.

HORST: What?

MAX: You'll drop the rock.

HORST: No I won't. I'm holding it, I'm holding it. What
right do you have . . .?

MAX: You were at the stones?

HORST: Yes.

MAX: Was it harder than this?

HORST: I suppose so.

MAX: People became ill?

HORST: Yes.

MAX: Die?

HORST:. Yes.

MAX: Guards beat you if you didn't work hard enough?

HORST: Yes.

MAX: [*proudly*] So?

HORST: So? So what?

MAX: So, it was dangerous.

HORST: This isn't?

MAX: No. No-one gets ill here. Look at all those blokes moving rocks over there. [*He points off.*] They look healthier than most. No-one dies. The guards don't beat you, because the work is totally non-essential. All it can do is drive you mad.

HORST: That's all?

MAX: Yes.

HORST: Then maybe the other was better.

MAX: No, I worked it out! This is the best work in the camp, if you keep your head, if you have someone to talk to.

HORST: Ah! I see! Someone to talk to! Don't you think you should have asked me . . .?

MAX: Asked you what?

HORST: If I wanted to move rocks, if I wanted to talk to you . . .

MAX: Didn't have a chance. They moved you.

HORST: Thank heaven.

MAX: Your new barracks, is it all pink triangles?

HORST: Yes. They're arresting more queers each day; they keep pouring into the camp. Is yours all yellow stars now?

MAX: Yes.

HORST: Good. You might go all religious. There was an old man at the stones. A rabbi. Really kind. It's not easy being kind here. He was. Kind to me. None of the other yellow stars want to acknowledge a pink triangle. We're not good enough to suffer with them. But this man was so godly. I thought of you.

MAX: Why?

HORST: Maybe if you knew him you could be proud of your star. You should be proud of *something*.

MAX: Don't keep looking at me. As long as they don't see us looking at each other, they can't tell we're talking.

[*Silence.*]

HORST: Where do the bodies come from?

MAX: What bodies?

HORST: The ones in the pit?

MAX: The fence. The hat trick.

HORST: Oh. What's that?

MAX: Sometimes a guard throws a prisoner's hat against the fence. He orders him to get the hat. If he doesn't get the hat, the guard will shoot him. If he does get the hat, he'll be electrocuted.

HORST: I'm really going to like it here. Thanks a lot.

MAX: I'm really doing you a favour.

HORST: A favour! You just want someone to talk to so you won't go mad. And I'm the only one who knows your secret.

MAX: What secret?

HORST: That you're a pink triangle.

MAX: It's not a secret.

HORST: If it's not a secret, wear one.

MAX: No. I'm a Jew now.

HORST: You are not.

MAX: They think I am.

HORST: But it's a lie.

MAX: It's a clever lie.

HORST: You're mad.

MAX: I thought you'd be grateful.

HORST: That's why you like this job. It can't drive you mad. You're already there.

MAX: I spent money getting you here.

HORST: Money?

MAX: Yes. I bribed the guard.

HORST: Where'd you get money?

MAX: My uncle sent me some. First letter I ever got from him. He didn't sign it, but it had money in it.

HORST: And you bribed the guard?

MAX: Yes.

HORST: For me?

MAX: Yes.

HORST: Used *your* money.

MAX: Yes.

HORST: You'll probably never get money again.

MAX: Probably not.

HORST: You are mad.

MAX: I thought you'd be grateful.

HORST: You should have asked me first.

MAX: How could I ask you? We're in separate barracks. Do you think it's easy to bribe a guard? It's complicated. It's dangerous. He could have turned on me. I took a risk. Do you think I didn't? I took a risk. I thought you'd be grateful.

HORST: I'm *not* grateful. I liked cutting stones. I liked that old rabbi. This is insane. Twelve hours of this a day? I'll be crazy in a week. Like you. Jesus!

MAX: I'm sorry I did it.

HORST: *You're* sorry.

MAX: You haven't got this camp sorted out, that's all. You don't know what's good for you. This is the best job to have.

HORST: Moving rocks back and forth for no reason. Next to a pit with dead bodies and a fence that can burn you to dust. The *best* job to have?

MAX: Yes! Why don't you understand?

HORST: I don't want to understand. I don't want to talk to you.

MAX: You have to talk to me.

HORST: Why?

MAX: I got you here to talk.

HORST: Well, hard luck. I don't want to talk. Move your rocks, and I'll move mine. Just don't speak to me.

[*They both move their rocks. A long silence.*]

MAX: I thought you'd be grateful.

[*Blackout*]

SCENE TWO

The same. Three days later.
MAX *and* HORST *are moving rocks. It is very hot. Their shirts lie on the ground. A long silence.*

HORST: It's so hot. Burning hot.
[*Silence.*]

MAX: You talked to me.

HORST: Weather talk, that's all.

MAX: After three days of silence.

HORST: *Weather* talk. Everyone talks about the weather. [*Silence.*] Anyhow.
[*Silence.*]

MAX: Did you say something?

HORST: No.
[*Silence.*]
Anyhow.

MAX: Anyhow?

HORST: Anyhow. Anyhow, I'm sorry. [*He stands still.*] Sometimes in this place, I behave like everyone else — bloody awful. Cut off, mean, not human, I'm sorry. You were doing me a favour. This is a good place to be. And the favour won't work unless we talk, will it?

MAX: Move!

HORST: What?

MAX: Talk while you're moving. Don't stop. They can see us.

HORST: [*starting to move the rock again*] It's hard to talk when you're going one way and I'm going the other. God, it's hot. [*Silence.*] Somebody died last night.

MAX: Where?

HORST: In my barracks. A Moslem.

MAX: An Arab?

HORST: No. A Moslem. That's what they call a dead person
         who walks. You know, one of those blokes who
         won't eat any more, won't talk any more, just
         wanders around waiting to really die.

MAX: I've seen them.

HORST: So one really died. In my barracks. [*Silence.*] God,
         it's hot.

                    [*Silence.*]

MAX: We'll miss the Olympics.

HORST: The what?

MAX: Olympics. Next month. In Berlin.

HORST: I knew there was a reason I didn't want to be here.

MAX: Perhaps they'll release us?

HORST: For the *Olympics?*

MAX: As a good will gesture. It *is* possible, don't you
         think?

HORST: I think it's not.

                    [*Silence.*]

MAX: Heard a rumour.

HORST: What?

MAX: Sardines tonight.

HORST: Don't like sardines.

MAX: It's only a rumour.

                    [*Silence.*]

HORST: God, it's hot.

                    [*Silence.*]

MAX: Very.

                    [*Silence.*]

HORST: Very what?

                    [*Silence.*]

MAX: Very hot.

                    [*Silence.*]

HORST: Suppose . . .

                    [*Silence.*]

MAX: What?

                    [*Silence.*]

HORST: Suppose after all this . . . [*Silence.*] We have nothing
to talk about.

> [*A loud bell rings.* MAX *and* HORST *put
> down their rocks and stand at attention,
> staring straight ahead.*]

Shit! I'd rather be moving rocks than standing in
the sun. Some rest period.

MAX: It's part of their plan.

HORST: What plan.

MAX: To drive us mad.

> [*Silence.*]

Was I awful to bring you here?

HORST: No.

MAX: I was, wasn't I?

HORST: No.

MAX: I had no right . . .

HORST: Stop it. Stop thinking how awful you are. Come on,
don't get depressed. Smile. [*Silence.*] You're not
smiling.

MAX: You can't see me.

HORST: I can feel you.

MAX: I wish we could look at each other.

HORST: I can feel you.

MAX: They hate it if anyone looks at each other.

HORST: I've been looking at you all morning.

MAX: Yeah?

HORST: You look sexy.

MAX: Me?

HORST: Without your shirt.

MAX: No.

HORST: Come off it. You know you're sexy.

MAX: No.

HORST: Liar.

> [MAX *smiles.*]

MAX: Of course I'm a liar.

HORST: Sure.

MAX: I've always been sexy.

HORST: Uh-huh.

MAX: Since I was a kid.

HORST: Yes?

MAX: Twelve. I got into a lot of trouble when I was . . .

HORST: Twelve?

MAX: Twelve.

HORST: Your body's beautiful.

MAX: I take care of it. I exercise.

HORST: What?

MAX: At night I do press-ups and knee bends in the barracks.

HORST: After twelve hours of moving rocks?

MAX: Yes. I worked it out. You got to keep your entire body strong. By yourself. That's how you survive here. You should do it.

HORST: I don't like to exercise.

MAX: You're a nurse.

HORST: For other people, not myself.

MAX: But you have to think of survival.

HORST: Sleep. I think of sleep. That's how I survive. Or I think of nothing. [*Silence.*] That frightens me. When I think of nothing.
> [*Silence.*]

MAX: You body's nice too.

HORST: It's OK. Not great.

MAX: No, it's nice.

HORST: Not as nice as yours.

MAX: No. But it's OK.

HORST: How do you know?

MAX: I've been looking too.

HORST: When?

MAX: All day.

HORST: Yes?

MAX: Yes.
> [*Silence.*]

HORST: Listen, do you . . .?

MAX: What?

HORST: Miss . . .

MAX: What?

HORST: You know.

MAX: No I don't.

HORST: Everyone misses it.

MAX: No.

HORST: Everyone in the camp.

MAX: No.

HORST: They go crazy missing it.

MAX: No.

HORST: Come on. No one can hear us. You're not a yellow star with me, remember? Do you miss it?

MAX: I don't want . . .

HORST: What?

MAX: To miss it.

HORST: But do you?

> [*Silence.*]

MAX: Yes.

HORST: Me too. [*Silence.*] We don't have to.

MAX: What?

HORST: Miss it. [*Silence.*] We're here together. We don't have to miss it.

MAX: We can't look at each other. We can't touch.

HORST: We can feel. . .

MAX: Feel what?

HORST: Each other. Without looking. Without touching. I can feel you right now. Next to me. Can you feel me?

MAX: No.

HORST: Come on. Don't be afraid. No one can hear us. Can you feel me?

MAX: Maybe.

HORST: No one's going to know. It's all right. Feel me.

MAX: Maybe.

HORST: Feel me.

MAX: It's so hot.

HORST: I'm touching you.

MAX: No.

HORST: I'm touching you.

MAX: It's burning.

HORST: I'm kissing you.

MAX: Burning.

HORST: Kissing your eyes.

MAX: Hot.

HORST: Kissing your lips.

MAX: Yes.

HORST: Mouth.

MAX: Yes.

HORST: Inside your mouth.

MAX: Yes.

HORST: Neck.

MAX: Yes.

HORST: Down . . .

MAX: Yes.

HORST: Down . . .

MAX: Yes.

HORST: Chest. My tongue . . .

MAX: Burning.

HORST: Your chest.

MAX: Your mouth.

HORST: I'm kissing your chest.

MAX: Yes.

HORST: Hard.

MAX: Yes.

HORST: Down...

MAX: Yes.

HORST: Down . . .

MAX: Yes.

HORST: Your cock.

MAX: Yes.

HORST: Do you feel my mouth?

MAX: Yes. Do you feel my cock?

HORST: Yes. Do you feel . . .?

MAX: Do you feel . . .?

HORST: Mouth.

MAX: Cock.

HORST: Cock.

MAX: Mouth.

HORST: Do you feel my cock?

MAX: Do you feel my mouth?

HORST: Yes.

MAX: Do you know what I'm doing?

HORST: Yes. Can you taste what I'm doing?
MAX: Yes.
HORST: Taste.
MAX: Feel.
HORST: Together ...
MAX: Together ...
HORST: Do you feel me?
MAX: I feel you.
HORST: I see you.
MAX: I feel you.
HORST: I have you.
MAX: I want you.
HORST: Do you feel me inside you?
MAX: I want you inside me.
HORST: Feel ...
MAX: I have you inside me.
HORST: Inside ...
MAX: Strong.
HORST: Do you feel me thrust ...?
MAX: Hold.
HORST: Stroke ...
MAX: Strong ...
HORST: Oh ...
MAX: Strong ...
HORST: Oh ...
MAX: Strong ...
HORST: I'm going to ...
MAX: Strong ...
HORST: Do you feel ...? I'm going to ...
MAX: I feel us both.
HORST: Do you ...?
MAX: Oh yes ...
HORST: Do you ...?
MAX: Yes. Yes.
HORST: Feel ...
MAX: Yes. Strong ...
HORST: Feel ...
MAX: More ...
HORST: Ohh ...

MAX: Now ...

HORST: Yes ...

MAX: Now! [*He gasps.*] Oh! Oh! My God!
[*He has an orgasm.*]

HORST: Ohh ...! Now! Ohh ...!
[*He has an orgasm. Silence.*]
Oh. [*Silence.*] Did you?

MAX: Yes. You?

HORST: Yes.
[*Silence.*]

MAX: You're a good fuck.

HORST: So are you. [*Silence.*] Max?

MAX: What?

HORST: We did it — fucking guards, fucking camp — we
did it! They're not going to kill us. We made love.
We were real. We were human. We made love.
They're not going to kill us.
[*Silence.*]

MAX: I never ...

HORST: What?

MAX: Thought we'd ...

HORST: What?

MAX: Do it in three minutes.
[*They laugh. The bell rings. They pick up
their rocks and resume moving them from
one side to the other.*]

[*Blackout*]

SCENE THREE
The same. Two months later.
MAX *and* HORST *are moving rocks. They are both
walking slowly.*

HORST: I'm going insane.
[*Silence.*]
I'm going insane.
[*Silence.*]

I'm going insane. I dream about rocks. I close my
eyes and I'm moving rocks. Rocks never end. Never
end.

[*Silence.*]

I'm going insane.

MAX: Think of something else.

HORST: I can't think. I've been up all night. *That's* why I'm
going insane.

MAX: Up all night?

HORST: Come on, didn't you hear? Our barracks had to
stand outside all night.

MAX: No.

HORST: Yes. We stood at attention all night long.
Punishment.

MAX: What for?

HORST: Someone in our barracks killed himself.

MAX: A Moslem?

HORST: Of course not. It doesn't mean anything if a Moslem
kills himself, but if a person who's still a person
commits suicide, well ... it's a kind of defiance,
isn't it? They hate that. It's an act of free will. Not
my way. But for some. So we were all punished.

MAX: I'm sorry.

HORST: Sure. Yellow star is sorry.

[*Silence.*]

MAX: Heard a rumour.

HORST: Sardines?

MAX: Yes.

HORST: I hate sardines! I hate all food. Scraps. Sardine
scraps. That's all we get anyhow. Not worth eating.
Didn't know you could have sardine scraps.
[*Silence.*] I'm going insane.

MAX: All right. You're going insane. I'm sorry. It's my
fault.

HORST: What do you mean, *your* fault?

MAX: For bringing you here. Because you make me feel so
guilty. And you should. This job *is* the worst. I got
it wrong. I'm sorry.

HORST: I'm glad to be here.

MAX: Of course.

HORST: I am.

MAX: How can you be?

HORST: That's my secret. [*Pause.*] Maybe if I closed my eyes
. . .

MAX: Heard a rumour.

HORST: What?

MAX: We may get potatoes.

HORST: When?

MAX: Tomorrow.

HORST: I don't believe it.

MAX: They said so in my barracks.

HORST: Who's they?

MAX: Some blokes.

HORST: Are they sexy?

MAX: Shut up.

HORST: You should be with us, where you belong.

MAX: No. But you shouldn't be *here*.

HORST: I want to be here.

MAX: Why would you want to be here — are you insane?

HORST: Of course I'm insane. I'm trying to tell you I'm
insane. And I want to be here.

MAX: Why?

HORST: Because. Because I love rocks. [*Pause.*] Because I
love you. [*Silence.*] I do. I love you. Isn't that silly?
When I'm not dreaming about rocks, I'm dreaming
about you. For the past six weeks, I've dreamt about
you. It helps me get up. It helps me make sure my
bed is perfectly made so I'm not punished. It helps
me push to get a place in the toilet line. It helps me
eat the stinking food. It helps me put up with the
constant fights in the barracks. Knowing I'll see
you. At least out of the corner of my eyes. In passing.
It's a reason to live. So I'm glad I'm here.

> [MAX *is at one pile of rocks, moving them
> into symmetrical piles.*]

What are you doing?

MAX: Arranging these neatly. We've become sloppy.

They can beat you for it. [*Silence.*] Don't love me.

HORST: It makes me happy. It doesn't harm anyone. It's my secret.

MAX: Don't love me.

HORST: It's my secret. And I have a signal. No one knows it. When I rub my left eyebrow at you, like this . . . [*He rubs his left eyebrow.*] It means I love you. Bet you didn't know that. I can even do it in front of the guards. No-one knows. It's my secret. [*He starts to cough.*] It's cold. It was better hot. I don't like it cold.

MAX: Don't love me.

HORST: I can't help it.

MAX: I don't want anybody to love me.

HORST: Too bad.

MAX: I can't love anybody back.

HORST: Who's asking you to?

MAX: Queers aren't meant to love. I know. I thought I loved someone once. He worked in my father's factory. My father paid him to go away. He went. Queers aren't meant to love. They don't want us to. You know who loved me? That boy. That dancer, I don't remember his name. But I killed him. See — queers aren't meant to love. I'll kill you too. Hate me. That's better. Hate me. Don't love me.

HORST: I'll do what I want to do. It isn't any of your business, anyhow. I'm sorry I told you.

MAX: I'm sorry I brought you here.

> [*He finishes arranging the rocks. He returns to moving the rocks. Silence.* HORST *starts to cough again.*]

Why are you coughing?

HORST: Because I like to.

MAX: Are you catching cold?

HORST: Probably. Up all night. In the wind.

MAX: Winter's coming.

HORST: I know. [*Silence.*] I just want to close my eyes . . .

MAX: Heard a rumour.

HORST: I don't care.

MAX: Don't you want to hear it?

HORST: Stuff your rumours.

> [*He coughs again. He slips. He drops the rock and falls to the ground.*]

MAX: Horst!

> [*He puts down his rock.*]

HORST: Shit.

> [MAX *starts towards him.*]

Don't move! He's watching. The guard. Don't help me. If you help me, they'll kill you. Get back to your rock. Do you hear me, get back!

> [MAX *returns, picks up his rock, but stands looking at* HORST. HORST *is coughing. He looks up at* MAX.]

Move!

> [MAX *moves the rock.*]

Right. I'm all right. I'll get up. I'll get up. Don't ever help me. [*He pulls himself up.*] I'm up. It's all right. [*He picks up his rock.*] These bloody things get heavier and heavier. [*He starts to move the rock.*] The guard was watching. He'd kill you if you helped me. Never notice. Never watch. Remember? I love you. But I won't help you if *you* fall. Don't you dare help me. You don't even love me, so why are you going to help? We save *ourselves.* Do you understand? Do you?

MAX: Yes. I understand.

HORST: Promise me. Come on. Promise me. We save ourselves.

MAX: All right.

HORST: Promise me!

MAX: Yes!

HORST: You're a fool. I don't love you any more. It was just a passing fancy. I love myself. Poor you, you don't love anybody. [*Silence.*] It's getting cold. Winter's coming.

> [*They walk, moving the rocks in silence.*]

[*Blackout*]

SCENE FOUR

The same. Two months later.

MAX *and* HORST *are moving rocks. They wear jackets.* HORST *is slower than ever, as if dazed. He is holding the rocks with difficulty. He has a coughing spell.*

MAX: You have a barracks leader.
   [HORST's *coughing continues.*]
   He can get you medicine.
   [*The coughing continues.*]
   He can try to get you medicine.
   [*The coughing continues.*]
   You must ask him.
   [*The coughing continues.*]
   You must get help.
   [*The coughing continues.*]
   You must stop coughing . . .!
   [*The coughing spell slowly subsides.*]
HORST: It doesn't matter.
MAX: If you're nice to the Kapo . . .
HORST: It doesn't matter.
MAX: Some sort of medicine.
HORST: What for? The cough? How about the hands?
MAX: I told you what to do. Exercise.
HORST: They're frostbitten.
MAX: So exercise.
HORST: It doesn't matter.
MAX: Every night, I move my fingers up and down, one at a time, for a half hour. I don't do press-ups any more. Just fingers.
HORST: It doesn't matter.
MAX: You're losing weight.
HORST: I don't like sardines.
MAX: I don't know what's happening. I don't understand you.
HORST: It doesn't matter.
MAX: I can't talk you into anything. I can do that. I can talk people into things.

HORST: Can't talk me into sardines.
> [HORST *starts to cough again. It goes on for
> a minute, then subsides.*]

MAX: It's getting worse.

HORST: It's getting colder.

MAX: You need medicine.

HORST: Stop nagging me.

MAX: See your Kapo.

HORST: He doesn't care.

MAX: Ask him.

HORST: He wants money.

MAX: Are you sure?

HORST: It doesn't matter.

MAX: I thought you cared about yourself.

HORST: You don't know anything.

MAX: I thought you loved yourself.

HORST: It's too cold.

MAX: You know what? [*Silence.*] You know what? You're
turning into a Moslem.

HORST: You turned into a Jew. I turned into a Moslem.

MAX: It's not funny.

HORST: Moslems don't make jokes. So I'm not a Moslem.
I'm just cold.

MAX: I'm scared.

HORST: Who isn't?

MAX: For you.

HORST: Be scared for yourself.

MAX: Why don't you listen to me?

HORST: Moslems don't listen.

MAX: You're not a Moslem.

HORST: Who said I was?

MAX: I didn't mean it. You're not a Moslem.

HORST: You're not a Jew.

MAX: Can't you ever forget that?

HORST: If I forget that . . . then . . . I am a Moslem.
> [*The bell rings. They both drop their rocks
> and stand at attention, side by side, looking
> straight ahead.*]

Look, I'm just cold. My fingers are numb. I can't

     stop coughing. I hate food. That's all. Nothing
     special. Don't get upset.
MAX: I want you to care.
HORST: I would. If I was warm.
MAX: I'll warm you.
HORST: You can't.
MAX: I know how.
HORST: No. You don't.
MAX: I do. I'm good at it. You said so.
HORST: When?
MAX: I'm next to you.
HORST: Don't start.
MAX: I'll make love to you.
HORST: Not now.
MAX: Yes. Now.
HORST: I have a headache. I can't.
MAX: Don't joke.
HORST: Moslems don't joke.
MAX: You're not a Moslem.
HORST: You're not a Jew.
MAX: Forget that.
HORST: No.
MAX: I'll make love to you.
HORST: No.
MAX: I'll make you warm.
      [Pause.]
HORST: You can't.
MAX: You'll feel the warm ...
HORST: I can't.
MAX: You'll *feel* it.
      [Pause.]
HORST: In my fingers?
MAX: All over.
HORST: I can't.
MAX: I'm kissing your fingers.
HORST: They're numb.
MAX: My mouth is hot.
HORST: They're cold.
MAX: My mouth is on fire.

HORST: My fingers . . .

MAX: Are getting warm.

HORST: Are they?

MAX: They're getting warm.

HORST: I can't tell.

MAX: They're getting warm.

HORST: A little.

MAX: They're getting warm.

HORST: Yes.

MAX: My mouth is on fire. Your fingers are on fire. Your body's on fire.

HORST: Yes.

MAX: My mouth is all over you.

HORST: Yes.

MAX: My mouth is on your chest . . .

HORST: Yes.

MAX: Kissing your chest.

HORST: Yes.

MAX: Making it warm.

HORST: Yes.

MAX: Biting your nipple.

HORST: Yes.

MAX: Biting . . . into it . . .

HORST: Yes.

MAX: Harder . . . harder . . . harder . . .

HORST: Stop it! That hurts!

MAX: Harder . . .

HORST: No, stop it. I'm serious. You're hurting me.
        [*A pause.* MAX *catches his breath.*]

MAX: You pulled away.

HORST: Yes, I did.

MAX: It was exciting.

HORST: For *you* maybe. I don't try to hurt you.

MAX: I like being hurt. It's exciting.

HORST: It's not. Not when you're rough.

MAX: I'm not being rough.

HORST: Yes you are. Sometimes you are.

MAX: OK. So what? It's exciting.

HORST: Why'd you have to spoil it? You were making me warm. Why can't you be gentle?

MAX: I am.

HORST: You're not. You try to hurt me. You make me warm, and then you hurt me. I hurt enough. I don't want to feel *more* pain. Why can't you be gentle?

MAX: I am.

HORST: No, you're not. You're like them. You're like the guards. You're like the Gestapo. We stopped being gentle. I watched it, when we were on the outside. People made pain and called it love. I don't want to be like that. You don't make love to hurt.

MAX: I wanted to make you warm. That's all I wanted. I can't do anything right. I don't understand you. I used to do things right.

HORST: You still can.

MAX: People liked it when I got rough. Most. Not everybody. He didn't.

HORST: Who?

MAX: The dancer. But everyone else did. Just a little rough.

HORST: Did you like it?

MAX: I don't remember. I could never remember. I was always drunk. There was always coke. Nothing seemed to matter that much.

HORST: But some things do matter.

MAX: Not to you.

HORST: They do.

MAX: I don't understand you. All day long you've been saying nothing matters . . . your cough, your fingers . . .

HORST: They matter.

MAX: I don't understand anything anymore.

HORST: They all matter. I'm not a Moslem. You're not a Jew. My fingers are cold.

MAX: I want you to be happy.

HORST: Is that true?

MAX: I think so. I don't know. [*Pause.*] Yes.

HORST: Then be gentle with me.

MAX: I don't know how.

HORST: You know how.

MAX: You told me I don't.

HORST: I love you gentle. Love me gentle.

MAX: I don't know how.

HORST: Just hold me.

MAX: I'm afraid to hold you.

HORST: Don't be.

MAX: I'm afraid.

HORST: Don't be.

MAX: I'm going to drown.

HORST: Hold me. Please. Hold me.

MAX: OK. I'm holding you.

HORST: Are you?

MAX: Yes. You're in my arms.

HORST: Am I?

MAX: You're here in my arms. I promise. I'm holding you. You're here . . .

HORST: Touch me.

MAX: No.

HORST: Gently . . .

MAX: Here.

HORST: Are you?

MAX: Yes. Touching.

HORST: Gently.

MAX: Touching. Softly.

HORST: Warm me.

MAX: Softly.

HORST: Warm me . . . gently . . .

MAX: Softly . . . . I'm touching you softly . . . gently . . . you're safe . . . I'll keep you safe . . . and warm . . . you're with me now . . . you'll never be cold again . . . I'm holding you now . . . safe . . . and warm . . . as long as you're here, as long as you're with me, as long as I'm holding you, you're safe . . .

[*Blackout*]

SCENE FIVE
The same. Three days later.
MAX *is moving rocks.* HORST *is putting the rock pile into neat order.*

HORST: The air is fresh today. Clean.
    [HORST *starts to cough. He continues coughing, then stops.*]
MAX: It sounds better.
HORST: It does.
MAX: Loosening up.
HORST: It is.
MAX: The medicine is helping.
HORST: Yes. [*Silence.*] Thank you. [*Silence.*] Why don't you tell me?
MAX: Tell you what?
HORST: How you got it.
MAX: Told you. Spoke to my barracks leader. He took me to an officer.
HORST: Which one?
MAX: Some captain. The new one.
HORST: He's rotten.
MAX: You know him?
HORST: I've heard about him. You gave him money?
MAX: Yes.
HORST: I don't believe you.
MAX: Why?
HORST: You don't have any money.
MAX: My uncle sent me some.
HORST: No he didn't. He only wrote to you once.
MAX: He wrote to me again.
HORST: No. He didn't.
MAX: I didn't tell you.
HORST: Why not?
MAX: Because no one writes to *you*.
HORST: Your uncle wrote to you once.
MAX: He wrote to me again.
HORST: You're a liar.

MAX: Why don't you ever believe me?

HORST: Because I can tell when you're lying. You think you're so good at it. You're not. Your voice changes.

MAX: It what!

HORST: Changes. Sounds different.

MAX: Rubbish.

HORST: How'd you get it?

MAX: I gave him money.

HORST: Liar.

[*Silence.*]

MAX: Hey ...

HORST: What?

MAX: Guess who I saw?

HORST: Where?

MAX: In my barracks.

HORST: Marlene Dietrich.

MAX: No. My landlord. From Berlin. Rosen.

HORST: Oh.

MAX: Nice man.

HORST: I thought you hated him.

MAX: Yes, I used to think he was what I was supposed to think he was.

HORST: What was that?

MAX: A lousy Jew.

HORST: He probably thought you were a lousy queer.

MAX: Probably.

HORST: Now he thinks you're not a queer. It's a shame.

MAX: It's not a shame. Don't start again.

[HORST *has a coughing spell.*]

You *are* taking the medicine?

[*The coughing subsides.*]

HORST: Of course I am. [*Silence.*] Of course I am, Max, I'm glad you got it.

MAX: So am I.

[*Silence.*]

HORST: Wish I knew how, though.

MAX: I told you.

HORST: You're a liar.

MAX: I am not.

HORST: It's just that . . . you don't have any money. Your
          uncle doesn't write to you. I know. It's silly for us to
          have secrets.
               [*Silence.*]
MAX: Higher or lower?
HORST: What?
MAX: Does my voice get higher or lower?
HORST: Just different.
               [*Silence.*]
MAX: I never met anyone like you. Can't make you believe
          anything.
HORST: How'd you get it?
MAX: You're never going to let up, are you?
HORST: Probably not.
MAX: Won't just be grateful.
HORST: Am I ever?
MAX: Suppose you don't like the answer.
HORST: I'll chance it.
MAX: Then when I tell you, you'll nag me about *that*.
HORST: You chance it.
MAX: I went down on him.
HORST: What?
MAX: You heard me?
HORST: No I didn't.
MAX: You wanted to know. I told you you wouldn't like
          it.
HORST: That SS captain?
MAX: Uh-huh.
HORST: He's the worst bastard in the . . .
MAX: I know.
HORST: You went down on him?
MAX: I had to. I didn't have any money.
HORST: You touched him?
MAX: No. I just went down on him. That's what he
          wanted. And I needed the medicine.
HORST: I'd rather cough.
MAX: No you wouldn't.
HORST: That bastard?
MAX: Yes.

HORST: Is he queer?

MAX: Who knows? Just felt like it, maybe. Of course, he could be queer. You don't like to think about that, do you? You don't want *them* to be queer.

HORST: No, I don't.

MAX: That's silly.

[*Silence.*]

HORST: Well, for once, you're right. It is silly. There *are* queer Nazis. And queer saints. And queer geniuses. And queer mediocrities. No better, no worse. Just people. I really believe that. That's why I signed Hirschfield's petition. That's why I ended up here. That's why I'm wearing this triangle. That's why you should be wearing it.

MAX: Do you think that captain would let a queer go down on him? Of course not. Somebody straight, yes. Even a Jew. But not a queer. That would mean maybe he was a queer. And even though maybe he *is,* he hates them more than . . .

HORST: Jews.

MAX: Yes. He'd kill me if he knew I was queer. My yellow star got your medicine.

HORST: Who needs it?

MAX: Then give it back. Throw it away. Throw it away, why don't you? And die. And you *will* die. In time. The cough will start it . . . I'm tired of being told I should have a pink triangle.

HORST: Well . . . [*Silence.*] He remember you?

MAX: Who?

HORST: Rosen?

MAX: Yes. He said I owed him rent.

HORST: What's Berlin like? Did he say?

MAX: Worse.

HORST: I miss it.

MAX: Yes. [*Pause.*] Ever go to The Silhouette?

HORST: Yes.

MAX: I never saw you there.

HORST: You weren't looking.

MAX: Greta's Club?

HORST: No.

MAX: Good. You had taste. The White Mouse?

HORST: Sometimes.

MAX: Surprised you never saw me.

HORST: What were you wearing?

MAX: Things that came off. I was conspicuous.

HORST: Why?

MAX: Because I was always making a fool of myself. I'm told. I don't remember. Did you sunbathe?

HORST: I loved to sunbathe.

MAX: In the nude?

HORST: Of course.

MAX: By the river.

HORST: That's right.

MAX: And you *never* saw me?

HORST: Well, actually, I did. I saw you by the river. You were making a fool of yourself. And I said some day, I'll be at Dachau with that man, moving rocks.

MAX: I didn't like Berlin. I mean, I wasn't happy. I was poor. I wasn't used to that. And always in a daze. And always scared. But I like it now. I miss it.

> [*He finishes straightening the rocks and resumes moving them.*]

HORST: We'll go back some day.

MAX: When we get out of here?

HORST: Yes.

MAX: We will, won't we?

HORST: We have to. Don't we?

MAX: Yes. Horst?

HORST: What?

MAX: We can go back together.

> [*An* SS CAPTAIN *enters. The* CORPORAL *is with him.* MAX *and* HORST *look up for a second, then continue with their task. The* CAPTAIN *stares at* MAX *for a long time, then* HORST, *then* MAX *again.*]

CAPTAIN: [*to* MAX] You. Jew.

> [MAX *stands still.*]

MAX: Yes sir?

CAPTAIN: Feeling better?
MAX: Sir?
CAPTAIN: Your cold?
MAX: Yes sir.
CAPTAIN: Remarkable.
MAX: Yes sir.
CAPTAIN: You seem so strong.
MAX: Yes sir.
CAPTAIN: Not ill at all.
MAX: No sir.
CAPTAIN: No?
MAX: Not now, sir.
CAPTAIN: Carry on.

> [MAX *resumes moving rocks. The* CAPTAIN
> *watches* MAX *and* HORST. *He paces up and
> down.* MAX *and* HORST *move the rocks. The*
> CAPTAIN *paces.* HORST *coughs. He catches
> himself, and tries to stifle it.*]

Ah.

> [HORST *stops the cough.*]

You. Pervert.

> [HORST *stiffens and stands still.*]

HORST: Yes sir?
CAPTAIN: Are you ill?
HORST: No sir.
CAPTAIN: You have a cough.
HORST: No sir.
CAPTAIN: I heard you cough.
HORST: Yes sir.
CAPTAIN: Something caught in your throat?
HORST: Yes sir.
CAPTAIN: From breakfast?
HORST: Yes sir.
CAPTAIN: Ah. Carry on.

> [HORST *resumes his work.* MAX *and* HORST
> *move the rocks. The* CAPTAIN *stands watch-
> ing them. He takes out a cigarette. The* COR-
> PORAL *lights it. The* CAPTAIN *smokes the*

> *cigarette and watches* MAX *and* HORST. MAX
> *and* HORST *continue moving rocks.* HORST
> *coughs again, attempting to strangle it, but
> the cough comes through.*]

CAPTAIN: You. Pervert.
> [HORST *stands still.*]
HORST: Yes sir.
CAPTAIN: You coughed.
HORST: Yes sir.
CAPTAIN: You're not well.
HORST: I am, sir.
CAPTAIN: I see. [*to* MAX] You. Jew.
> [MAX *stands still.*]
MAX: Yes sir.
CAPTAIN: Watch.
MAX: Watch, sir?
CAPTAIN: Yes. Watch. [*to* HORST] You.
HORST: Yes sir.
CAPTAIN: Put down that rock.
HORST: Yes sir.
> [*He puts down the rock.*]
CAPTAIN: Good. Now take off your hat.
> [*A long pause.*]
HORST: My hat, sir?
CAPTAIN: Yes. Your hat.
HORST: My hat, sir?
CAPTAIN: Your hat.
HORST: Yes sir.
> [HORST *removes his hat.* MAX'S *hand moves.*
> HORST *shoots him a warning stare.*]
CAPTAIN: [*to* MAX] You.
MAX: Yes sir.
CAPTAIN: Relax.
MAX: Yes sir.
CAPTAIN: And watch.
MAX: Yes sir.
CAPTAIN: [*to* HORST] You.
HORST: Yes sir.

CAPTAIN: Throw your hat away.

> [HORST *flings his hat on the ground.*]

Not there.

HORST: Not there, sir?

CAPTAIN: No. Pick it up.

HORST: Yes sir.

> [*He picks up his hat.*]

CAPTAIN: Throw it on the fence.

HORST: The fence, sir?

CAPTAIN: The fence.

> [HORST *starts to cough.*]

That's all right. We'll wait.

> [*The cough subsides.*]

Are you better?

HORST: Yes sir.

CAPTAIN: Nasty cough.

HORST: Yes sir.

CAPTAIN: On the fence. Now.

HORST: On the fence. Yes sir.

> [HORST *glances at* MAX — *another warning stare — then throws his hat on the fence. The fence sparks.*]

CAPTAIN: [*to* MAX] You.

MAX: Yes sir.

CAPTAIN: Are you watching?

MAX: Yes sir.

CAPTAIN: Good [*to* HORST] You.

HORST: Yes sir.

CAPTAIN: Get your hat. [*Silence.*] Did you hear me?

HORST: Yes sir.

CAPTAIN: Get your hat.

> [*The* CAPTAIN *motions to the* CORPORAL. *The* CORPORAL *points his rifle at* HORST.]

HORST: Now, sir?

CAPTAIN: Now.

HORST: Are you sure, sir?

CAPTAIN: Quite.

HORST: Could I do without my hat, sir?

CAPTAIN: No.

[HORST *is silent for a moment. He feels* MAX *watching, and gives him another quick glance, his eyes saying, 'don't move'. He turns to the* CAPTAIN.]

HORST: Yes sir.

[HORST *looks at* MAX. *He takes his hand and rubs his left eyebrow. He turns and stares at the* CAPTAIN. *The* CAPTAIN *waits. The* CORPORAL *is pointing his rifle.* HORST *turns towards the fence. He starts to walk very slowly to his hat. He almost reaches the fence when, suddenly, he turns and rushes at the* CAPTAIN. *He screams in fury. The* CORPORAL *shoots* HORST. HORST *continues to lunge at the* CAPTAIN. *His hand is out. He scratches the* CAPTAIN's *face. The* CORPORAL *shoots* HORST *in the back. He falls, dead.*]

[*Silence.*]

[*The* CAPTAIN *holds his face.*]

CAPTAIN: [*to* MAX] You. Jew.

[MAX *is silent.*]

You!

MAX: Yes sir.

CAPTAIN: I hope the medicine helped. [*He turns to leave, then turns back.*] Get rid of the body.

[*Silence.*]

MAX: Yes sir.

[*The* CAPTAIN *leaves. The* CORPORAL *points the rifle at* MAX, *lowers it, then walks off, after the* CAPTAIN.]

[MAX *stares at* HORST.]

[*Silence.*]

[MAX *opens his mouth to cry out. He can't.*]

[*Silence.*]

[MAX *walks to* HORST's *body. He tries to lift it. It is heavy. He manages to pull the body partly up,* HORST's *head resting against* MAX's *chest. He looks away. He takes*

HORST, *feet dragging on the ground,
towards the pit.*]
[*The bell rings.*]

No!

[*He looks up — off — at the* CORPORAL,
then back at HORST. *He stands at attention.*
HORST *starts to fall.* MAX *pulls him up. He
stands still, staring in front of him, holding
on to* HORST.]

It's OK. I won't drop you. I'll hold you. If I stand at
attention, I can hold you. They'll let me hold you. I
won't let you down.

[*Silence.*]

I never held you before.

[*Silence.*]

You're safe. I won't drop you.

[*Silence.*]

Don't worry about the rocks. I'll do yours too. I'll
move twice as many each day. I'll do yours too. You
don't have to worry about them.

[*Silence.*]

I won't drop you.

[*Silence.*]

You know what?

[*Silence.*]

Horst?

[*Silence.*]

You know what?

[*Silence.*]

I think . . .

[*Silence.*]

I think I love you.

[*Silence.*]

Shh! Don't tell anyone. Don't worry about the
rocks. I won't drop you. I promise . . . I think I loved
. . . I can't remember his name. A dancer. I think I
loved him too. Don't be jealous. Will I forget your
name? No-one else will touch the rocks. I think I
loved . . . some boy, a long time ago. In my father's

factory. Hans. That was his name. But the dancer. I
don't remember. Don't be jealous. I won't let you
drop.

[*Silence.*]

If I walk a little faster, I can do twice as many rocks a
day. I won't let you down.

[*Silence.*]

I won't let you drop.

[*Silence.*]

I love you.

[*Silence.*]

What's wrong with that?

[*Silence.*]

I won't let you drop. I won't let you drop.

[*Silence.*]

You know what I did? I got your medicine.

[*Silence.*]

Hey —

[*Silence.*]

I don't remember your name.

[*Silence.*]

Oh my God! This can't be happening.

[*He starts to cry. The bell rings. He drags*
HORST's *body to the pit. He throws it in the
pit. He turns and looks at the rocks. He
takes a deep breath. He walks over to the
rocks and picks one up. He moves it across
to the other side. He takes another deep
breath. He stands still.*]

One. Two. Three. Four. Five. [*He takes another
deep breath.*] Six. Seven. Eight. Nine. Ten.

[*He picks up a rock. He moves it across to
the other side.*]

[*He moves another rock.*]

[*He moves another rock.*]

[*He moves another rock.*]

[*He pauses. He takes a deep breath.*]

[*He moves another rock.*]

[*He moves another rock.*]

[*He stops. He tries to take another deep breath. He can't. His hand is trembling. He steadies his hand. He picks up another rock and starts to move it.*]

[*He stops. He drops the rock. He moves towards the pit.*]

[*He jumps into the pit.*]

[*He disappears.*]

[*A long pause.*]

[*He climbs out of the pit.*]

[*He holds* HORST's *jacket, with the pink triangle on it. He takes off his own jacket. He puts* HORST's *jacket on.*]

[*He turns and looks at the fence.*]

[*He walks into the fence.*]

[*The fence lights up. It grows brighter and brighter, until the light consumes the stage.*]

[*And blinds the audience.*]

THE END